POSSESSIONS™

Book Two

The Ghost Table

Gurgazon The Unclean

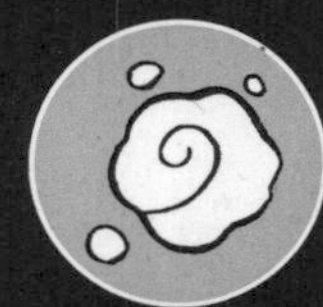

The Ice Field Lights

The Pale Lady

The Duke

The Sturmann Poltergeist aka "Polly"

Mr. Thorne

Ms. Llewellyn-Vane

Nasty and snide

So cold he died

Victim of pride

Haunted and fried

Nature defied

Extremely keen-eyed

Most satisfied

Book Two
The Ghost Table

WRITTEN & ILLUSTRATED BY

RAY FAWKES

DESIGN BY

KEITH WOOD

EDITED BY

JILL BEATON

Oni Press, Inc.
publisher Joe Nozemack
editor in chief James Lucas Jones
marketing director Cory Casoni
art director Keith Wood
operations director George Rohac
associate editor Jill Beaton
associate editor Charlie Chu
production assistant Douglas E. Sherwood

Possessions, Volume 2, March 2011. Published by Oni Press, Inc. 1305 SE Martin Luther King Jr. Blvd., Suite A, Portland, OR 97214.

Oni Press Inc.
1305 SE Martin Luther King Jr. Blvd.
Suite A
Portland, OR 97214

www.onipress.com

First Edition: March 2011
ISBN 978-1-934964-61-3

10 9 8 7 6 5 4 3 2 1

PRINTED IN THE U.S.A.

And this one's for Dodo.

Antarctica.

February, 1907.
One hundred and twenty miles from the South Pole.

Then you will die *alone.* Gregory and I are leaving!
CRACK!
Goodbye, Hjalmar!
We will live to try again!
Fools.

Two days later.
So--
so cold--
FLUMPF!

FOUR YEARS LATER.
Roald!
Roald, do you see that? What is that?
Wooooooooooooooo
It's nothing, Olav. A trick of the light on the snow.
Let's continue.

Twenty two years after that.
Let's see now--
puffy snow
fluffy snow
tall snow
icy snow
which is different from snowy ice--
Hey!
Hey, what--
Got what you came for?
Yes. Let's go.

The Llewellyn-Vane House for Captured Spirits and Ghostly Curiosities.
Today.
Ahhhh.
Nice and warm.
Whatever.
Do you think anyone will notice if this goes missing?
Gurgazon needs it for something.

Good Afternoon, Everybody.
SAY GOODBYE TO YOUR *FACE*, HUMAN!
EEE

WHOOSH
I have an announcement for you.
Mrs. Llewellyn-Vane will be hosting a dinner party in about an hour, and you will all be expected to attend.
VWEE!
You will, of course, be on best behavior.
Waitaminute, wait a minute.
BWORF!
An hour? And you're just telling us this now?
Mm, yes.
Who's coming?

Pardon?
Who's coming to dinner?
Oh, well, Ms. Carter-Hawthorne and her collection will be in attendance.
You have *got* to be kidding me.
WHAT
Who's that?
Who is Ms. Carter-Hawthorne?
BURY MY FACE INTO THE GROUND
I'M NOT GOING
All of you will attend.
I'll see you in an hour.
Somebody tell Gurgazon what's going on here!

Ms. Carter-Hawthorne is Ms. Llewellyn-Vane's chief rival collector.
She's an awful, awful woman.
But she's only half the problem.
Whenever she comes over, she brings her collection with her.
Four of the world's most irritating ghosts.. I'm not exaggerating here.
Horrible, just horrible.

Thorne. Looking dull and unwell, as usual.
Monsieur Le Comte.
The Hessian Volume.
FLIP!
"What's here? A portrait of a blinking idiot."
Mm.
Candle.
That's my name! Don't wear it out!
And Posy the Poltergeist. That's everyone then?

Don't worry. They can't possibly be bad enough to compete with Gurgazon.
Well, that's not really what I--
Gurgazon will be ten times worse!
That's probably true.
No, no. Gurgazon will be a *MILLION* times worse!
You're just going to go on, aren't you?
GURGAZON WILL MAKE THEM *IMPLODE WITH HORROR!*
HISSSSS
Anybody up for a game of checkers?

Soon.
OOH FANCY
AND EVERYTHING LOOKS GOOD TONIGHT
SHINE SHINE
How's my glow? Bright?
WAP WAP
Huh? You look the same as always.
Yes, but if I do--
BAM
this?

Okay.
That's pretty good.
It's hard to keep it going. Forget it.
Why bother getting fancy anyway? I thought you hate these guys.
We do, but it's nice to look nice.
Whatever.
Gurgazon has nothing to prove.
WHAP
BAM

Ms. Carter-Hawthorne and her collection are here, madam.
KISS KISS!
Amelia!
So good to see you! And you're looking wonderful!
Yes, yes. Here we are again.
Hmph.
So nice to see your little collection again, too!
I do hope your cook follows my instructions this time.
You know my diet is very specialized.
BUMP.
careful

Mr. Thorne, will you bring my spirits in?
At once, madam.
Ah, splendid! I really am so very proud of them.
Wait just a moment, please.
Step aside, servant!
Gurgazon waits for no lackey!
Shh.
Nobody shushes Gurgazon!
THE GLOVES ARE OFF NOW,
Now, Mr. Thorne!
GURGAZON *WILL* TEACH YOU *FEAR*!
GURGAZON WILL *RAVAGE* YOUR VERY--
SHOVE

Er--
All right, interlopers.
Having a good look?
GURGAZON DOESN'T *LIKE* BEING STARED AT.
GURGAZON WILL GIVE YOU 'TILL THE COUNT OF *ONE* TO STOP.
ONE.
I-- I don't believe it.

You really went and found yourself a pit demon.
I *demand* you tell me how you did it.
You know I *never* talk about my sources, dear.
HEY!
GURGAZON IS *RIGHT HERE!*
ALL RIGHT!
IT'S *GO* TIME!

Oh great.
Just what we need.
Another Llewellyn-Vane showoff.
You can say that again.
egh.
hnf.
grr.
Excuse me. Little girl?
Excuse me.
Do you mind perhaps shouting and throwing your lightning a little more quietly?
We are trying to have a conversation over here.

See you at dinner, my ghosties!
Be nice to our guests now!
Let go!
Gurgazon just wants to kill the head a *little*!
Do let her go, madame, so I may ***prove*** that ***this*** creature is no real pit demon.
GRRR!
YOU'LL BE LOOKING AT YOUR BRAIN FROM THE ***INSIDE,*** HEAD!

"Three can keep a secret, if two of them are dead."

Aargh! You're so--
You're all so annoying!
Look who's talking, Monsieur Cheap Fireworks.
Yeah!
NOBODY TALKS ABOUT MY FRIENDS LIKE THAT
Oh yes, *friends*, are you?
All such a *friendly* bunch.
No *real* ghost with an ounce of self-respect would behave the way you all do.
You aren't real ghosts!
You're just a bunch of pets!
Haha, right!

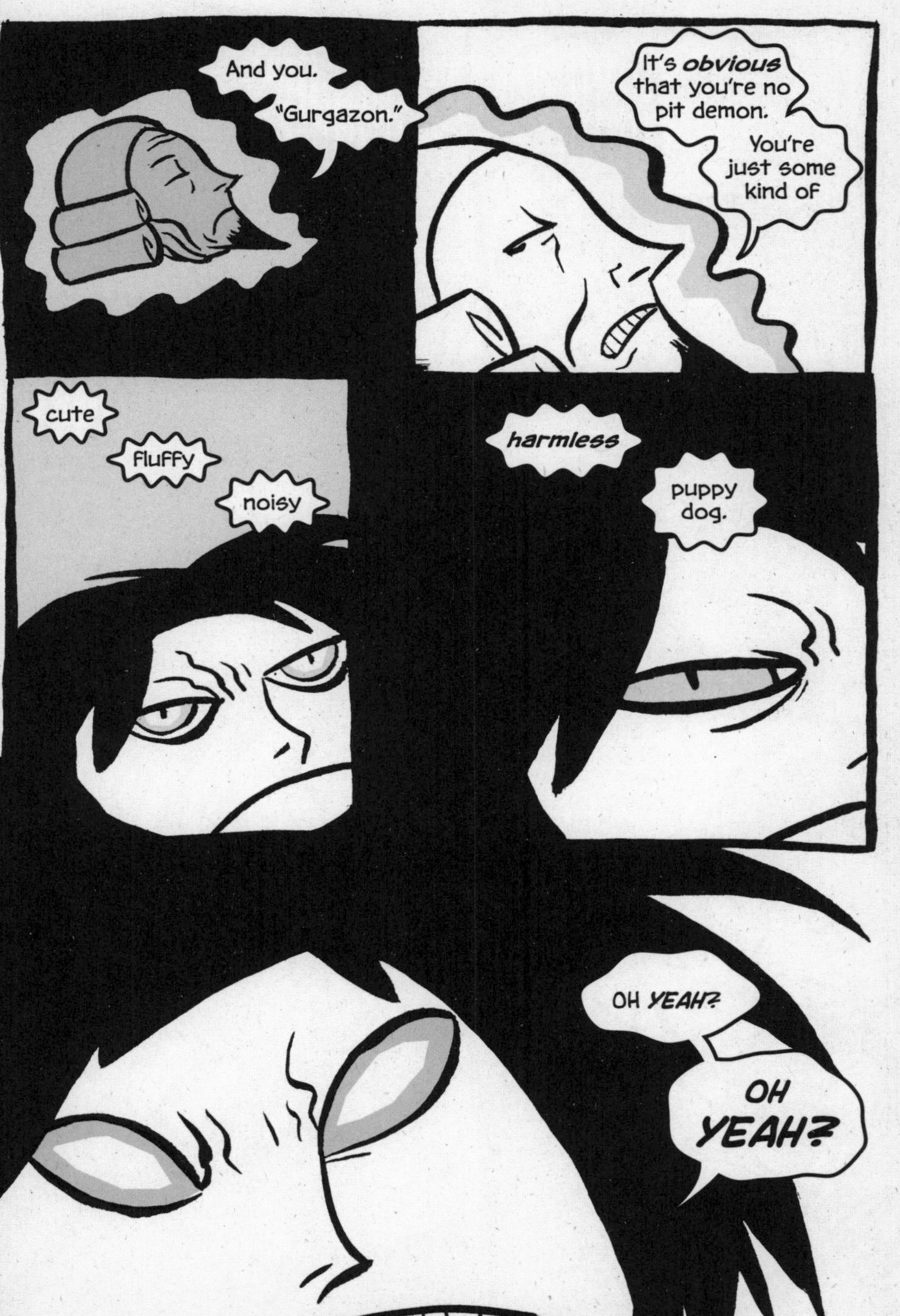
And you.
"Gurgazon."
It's *obvious* that you're no pit demon.
You're just some kind of
cute
fluffy
noisy
harmless
puppy dog.
OH *YEAH?*
OH YEAH?

WOULD A PUPPY DOG DO--
Hey, what the--
THIS?
SQUISH
STRETCH
I don't see why not.
Seriously.
GURGAZON THE UNCLEAN HAS NO COMPASSION! GURGAZON SPARES NO ONE!
THIS IS WHAT A "FRIEND" OF GURGAZON GETS!
LEAP!!
WHEN YOU HEAR THE SOUND OF WARNING
KIND OF SEEPING INTO ME

ee-hee-hee!
If you think Gurgazon is so harmless, maybe you want to come over here and give it a little hug?
JUST A NICE
LITTLE
W-well well--
WIPE WIPE
HSSSSS
TAKE IT AWAY
p-perhaps she is a pit demon after all.
Y-yeah--

PERHAPS?
GURGAZON WILL SHOW YOU SOME "PERHAPS"!
GRAB!

Oh man.
SMACK!
CRACK!
BEYOOO
TWANGG!
BASH!
POW!
BONK
BONK BONK
DING!
WE'RE GOING TO A BAD PARTY
Wait, wait! We are convinced!
Stop! Mercy!
I have information you might find useful!
INFORMATION ABOUT MISTER THORNE!
Really?
Really?
REALLY?
RILLY?
Really?

Spill it, head, or you'll be Gurgazon's early dinner.
LUX LIVES
And it better be something we don't *already* know.

Yes, yes!
We all know that Thorne is always there to prevent escape, no?
Always.
There must be something very special about this man, no?
And he visits often to advise our Ms. Carter-Hawthorne on security.
You see, we have trap spells cast on our home too.
But who cast them, hmm?
Was it the ladies?
You better be getting to a point.
Your butler is no ordinary human being!
He is--
He--

CLICK-
CLACK
Hello.
I trust you're all behaving yourselves?
CREEEEEEK
I brought refreshments.
TINKLE TINK
The dinner bell will ring shortly.
Lights, will you lead the guests to dinner when the time comes?
gulp
Sure.

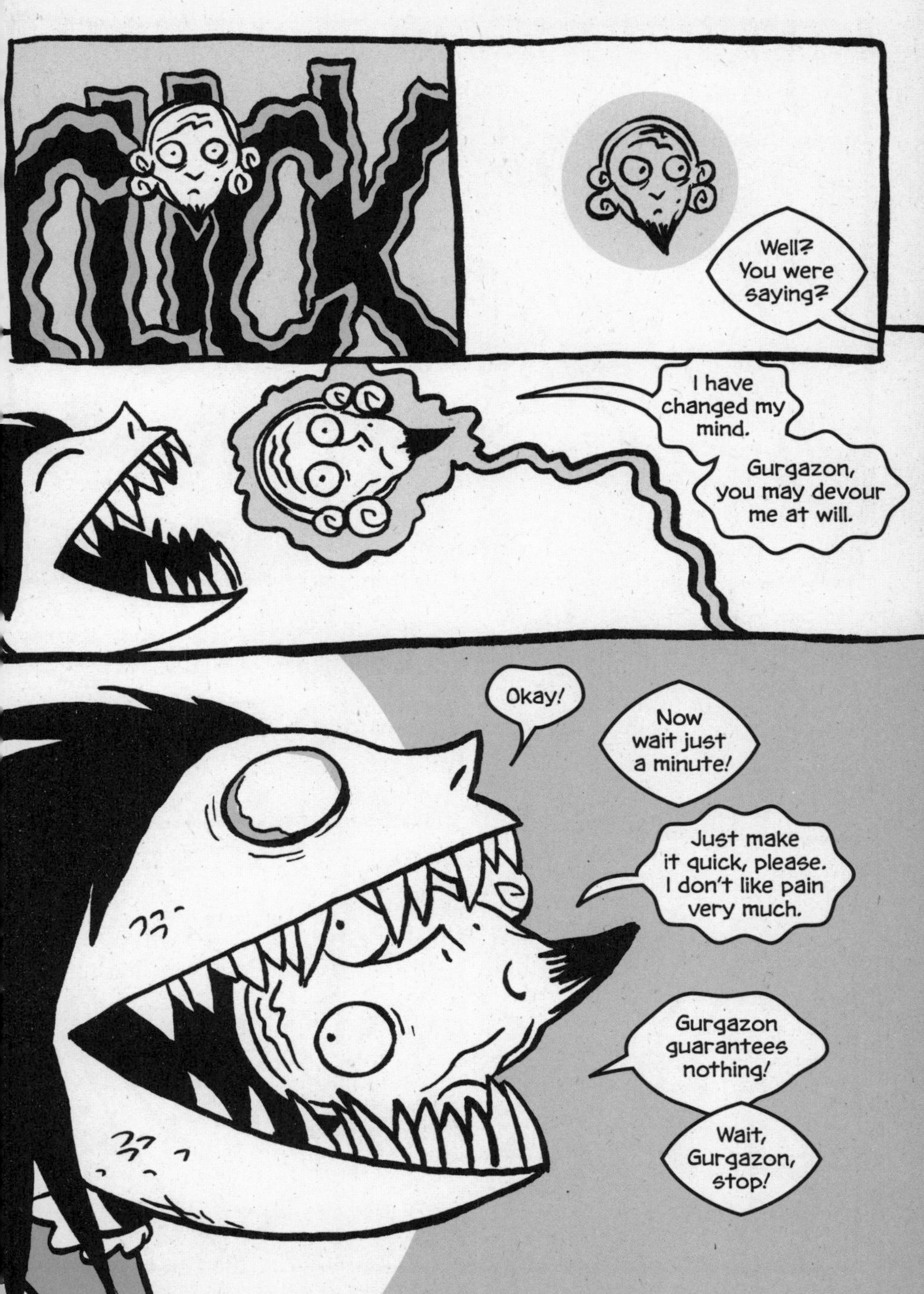
Well?
You were saying?
I have changed my mind.
Gurgazon, you may devour me at will.
Okay!
Now wait just a minute!
Just make it quick, please. I don't like pain very much.
Gurgazon guarantees nothing!
Wait, Gurgazon, stop!

Come on, Comte. Tell us what you know.
PULL!
What? I-- I cannot remember!
Who am I?
Oh, stop faking.
No, no, he's useless!
Gurgazon must destroy him!
Do I know you?
This is ridiculous. I give up.
Pardon me, Mademoiselle, but you look so familiar.
Were we, perhaps, sweeties?
He probably doesn't know anything anyway.
Just leave him be.
BUP!

Soon.
No hard feelings about that--
I mean, I know you--
He goaded you into acting like that.
I'm just trying to say I know you didn't *mean* it.
They're up to something.
Look at them.
whisper whisper
snicker
Dunderheads.
Gurgazon will discover their feeble plan and *mock* them.
SLORP!
Uh--
Hold this.
But--
CRASH!

DOO DEE DOO
Greetings, irritating intruders! Are you enjoying imposing on us?
Is-- Is this your way of attempting *chit-chat*?
Gurgazon laughs in comradely tones! Ha ha!
What creatures of mirth you are!
Gurgazon wishes to get down to brass tacks.
What's all the whispering? Are you trying to conceal your terror of Gurgazon?
It won't spoil the party if you let it show. Gurgazon *enjoys* your craven fear.

If you *must* know, we are finalizing the plans for our escape from this place.
Hey, Lights!
Check this out!
These cheap second-raters are funnier than they look!
Grr--
So, how do you propose to achieve that which Gurgazon cannot?
Because Gurgazon is far, *far*--
Yes, yes, *enough*.
Come, friends. *Ignore* the demon.
whisper whisper
Oh, sure! You don't *have* a plan do you?
This is just an attempt to annoy Gurgazon, isn't it?
Isn't it?

I guess you'll know for sure sooner or later, no?

Why don't you be a ***good*** little demon and go back to your friends?

Put on a fancy little dress and sit ***nicely*** for dinner.

Yes? Like a ***good*** little demon?

Pretending to hurt your friends but they will forgive you, no?

Because they know you are only ***faking*** being bad.

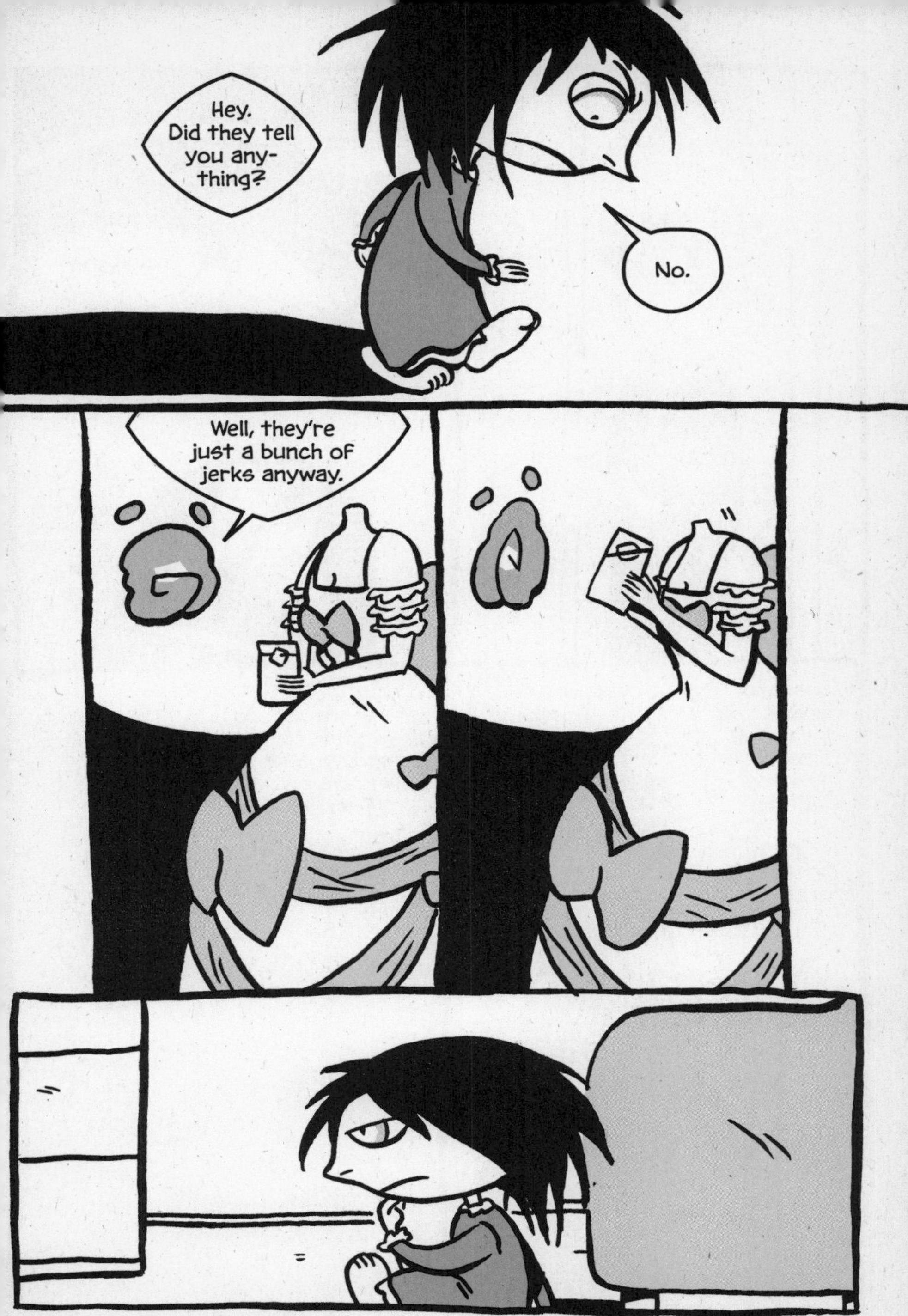
Hey.
Did they tell
you any-
thing?
No.
Well, they're
just a bunch of
jerks anyway.

CLICK-CLACK
Thorne.
Gurgazon.
Gurgazon realizes you are not an ordinary human being.
What makes you think that?
Gurgazon is going to discover your secrets and *defeat* you.
You think Gurgazon is *tamed?*
Gurgazon is *IMPOSSIBLE* to tame!
CLICK!

WELL I'M LOOKING FORWARD TO A NICE DINNER

SWEETLY REMINISCENT, SOMETHING MOTHER USED TO BAKE

Something's up with Gurgazon.

I think that creepy Comte said something that's bothering her.

I HOPE THEY'RE NOT BEING UNKIND TO HER

They are planning something.
What? Why?
And whatever it is they're planning, they're going to try to pin it on Gurgazon.
Only they know that.
But see how they provoke Gurgazon?
Gurgazon senses a set-up.
I think they're just plain rude.
No.
Gurgazon knows the difference between rude and crafty.

Well, if you're right, we'll back you up.
What's the plan?
Here's the *plan*:
The plan is *you* go to your "party."
Gurgazon needs no assistance.
Hmph.
I think we should work together on this.

Well, Gurgazon thinks you can stick it in your--

DINGADINGADING

If you'll all just follow me, please?

Outta my way, blob.
My name is *Lights*!
Watch it!
Come on, you idiots!
I'M CRAMPED
DON'T MAKE ME COME OVER THE
Hey!
YOU WATCH IT!
The *nerve*!

Ahem.

Hey, pretty classy.
Where do we sit?
Your table is over there.
Aw man. A ghost table? Why can't we sit with the grown-ups?

SHOVE!
SMACK
WHIZ!
THUMP THUMP
THUMP
THU
THUM
PTHBBBBT!
I think you know the answer to that question as well as I do.
Point taken.

No cutlery?
GURGAZON REQUIRES BLADES!
No, I don't think so.
grumble grumble

So--
Have any of you ever tried to *kill* Mr. Thorne?
Uh, don't you think we should talk about this some other time? He's right over *there*.
Etiquette is *irrelevant* to Gurgazon!
Gurgazon is an agent of hellish *chaos*!
I have.
I've tried to kill him.

You?
Yeah, just the once.
He was delivering a birthday gift for the old lady.
For once, I had a chance to sneak up behind him.
So--
WH-BOM!

That's it? You just *hit* him?
I hit him really, ***really*** hard!
Haha!
Then what happened?
Nothin'
He told me I was very rude.
Maybe he was ready for it.
HE'S ALWAYS ONE STEP AHEAD
Hmph.
This tells us nothing.
Anyone else?

Not me.
I kinda *like*
the guy.
I'M NOT
THE ONE
WHOOSH

WHIFF!
BLOCK!
SLUMP
So we have no evidence that he is actually *invulnerable* to attack.
Hey, I hit him as hard as I could!
Maybe he's just *lucky*.
Lucky, and at least a hundred years old.
Have you tried sunlight?
He gardens all the time.
Oh yes.
Gurgazon *remembers*.
Silver?
He handles Mrs. Llewellyn-Vane's good silverware.
AND FINE CHINA!

Fire?
He likes to barbecue.
RUNNING WATER?
He made the lemonade.
Hmm.
You'll *never* figure him out, demon.
Why don't you give Gurgazon a *hint*, head?
No. No, I think not.

ding ding
The Soup Course
OOOOOO
WAAAAAA
NYAAAA
EEEOOOOO

All right, ectoplasm.
Check *this* out.
OOOoWOoo
What are they doing *now*?
WOOooOO
I don't know. Showing off for the ladies?
OOoo-- What is this, vichyssoise?
These interlopers. They're clearly trying to drive Gurgazon over the edge.
Yeah, I can see how mad they're making you. I know how you feel.
GURGAZON MOCKS YOUR SYMPATHY.
--what?
Sorry. Gurgazon has habits.
Look at this recipe. It's all wrong!
Who made this soup? It's an embarrassment!
WOOoO ooWOo
nudge!

Hmm?
Oh!
WAAARGH!
EEEOOOEE
They mock Gurgazon for being "good."
And yet, look at *this.* Performing like circus ghosts.
Yeah, I noticed that.
So they're hypocrites.
Yes, but there is *more* to this.
Gurgazon is a demon of the lowest pits.
Gurgazon has seen ones like this head before.
Confidence men.
Courtiers.
WEEEAUU EEEGGGH
Manipulators.

See, with his type, it's always *crooked.* Never straight.
If they say they are one thing, it's because they are *another.*
Always hiding behind trickery and *lies.*
So they arrive tonight and this head starts right away, prodding Gurgazon into a frenzy of rage.
So?
So what he really wants--
What he really wants is--
Work with Gurgazon here.
He wants Gurgazon to *be--?*
--calm?
Precisely.
GET OUT
HOOOooOOo

OOH YES IT IS QUITE NICE. THE LEMONS ARE IN SEASON
And look at us. Behaving ourselves very nicely while the intruders howl and moan like ghosts should.
Currying favor with the demented old biddies, no doubt.
So you think we should act up too?
No, we wait.
But--
Timing is *everything*.
Oh.
Polly?
Follow Gurgazon's lead.
YES?
Do nothing until Gurgazon makes its move.
What are you going to do?
GURGAZON GIVES NO WARNING.
HISSSS

Relevé
ding
di
What in perdition is this?
BOOOooOO
Crayfish blanc-mange.
It looks like the inside of Gurgazon's *mind*.
You don't have to eat it.
Eat it?
POKE POKE
Gurgazon is considering *adopting* it.
EEEooOOOOEEE
I'D JUST AS SOON STAY SICK

YOOOWWLLLL
Hey, *Head.*
Are you getting bored yet?
YAWN
Because you're getting *boring.*
BLOOOOGAAAAH!

ding ding
Salad Course
Shouldn't we be *doing* something?
Don't worry.
First we let the head and his friends tire themselves out.
Is that all you've got, head?
The old *ladies* are scarier than you!
TWITCH

Oh my!
FLIP!
THUMP!
"Greedily she engorged without restraint, and knew not eating death;"
Lettuce, cucumber, radishes--
Gurgazon is beginning to understand.
You are attempting to *kill* Gurgazon.
GURGAZON IS INVULNERABLE TO NUTRITION!
Eat it or don't.
It doesn't matter to me.
Do you have "screaming helpless enemies" dressing?
Shouldn't you be glowing and gibbering like the others there?
You worry about carrying the plates, lackey, and Gurgazon will worry about when it's time to gibber.

ding di
Main Course
GGgurgle
AWOOoOO
Sigh.
Well, Mrs. Llewellyn-Vane, at least my ghosts are *trying.*
Yours don't look very energetic at all.
What? Were you *expecting* something from Gurgazon?
IS GURGAZON A PERFORMING MONKEY?
Gurgazon thought you just wanted us to enjoy a nice meal together.
As your *GUESTS.*

Polly.
These wrinkled humans want us to dance for our supper.
Shall we *dance?*
BAM
POP
YES

Oh dear!

DANCE WITH GURGAZON!

BOIN
PING!
CRAC
POWP
CRACK!
PING

SPROING
BOOM
BISH!

FWEE
WH
BIING
KAP

MEANWHILE...
TUCK
TUCK

BITE
MUNCH
MUNCH

SSSIP
AHH

Ahem.
ding ding
Dessert
Ee-hee
ooh-haha!
DROP
CRASH
TINKLE
SH
PLOP!
Ice Cream!
Now we're talking!

Well, Thorne, what do you think of Gurgazon's dance?
It's not for me to say.
Perhaps you'd like to ask--
RISE
them.
Oh, Mrs. Llewellyn-Vane!
Wonderful, wonderful!
The Specter Collectors' Society salutes you!
CLAP CLAP CLAP CLAP

Ladies, may I present:
The Carter-Hawthorne Collection!
6
6.5
8
They are rating us. All of this was a sham.
Hmm?
No, not a sham. *They* all had a nice dinner with some entertainment.
You knew all along.
And!
The Llewellyn-Vane collection!
10
9.5
0

Ms. Carter-Hawthorne wanted to prove, once and for all, that her collection--
that WE are superior.
We were to be rewarded with luxuries for our victory.
Fool.
YOU DARE TO JUDGE US? YOU RATE US?
GURGAZON IS ARMAGEDDON!
Lovely!
Oh, I wish I could get one!
What a dear!
Just look at those teeth!
ARMA--
That's enough, now.
The show is over for tonight.
Dessert is served.
ZIP

SNIFF SNIFF
Magic.
Powerful magic.
What are you?
I am the butler.

It's not fair.
You had a brand-new pit demon and you didn't tell me.
It's not *fair*.
You gotta admit, we put on a heck of a show.
I mean, when we all get together, we can really rip a joint up.
I'm just--
I think I'm just trying to say--
Think of what we could do if we all teamed up!
I mean--
Oh, give it a *rest*.

Come now, spirits.
It's time to go home.
Oh Amelia, please stay for tea. Don't be upset!
I think not.
Mister Thorne, please have our car brought around.
Yes, madam.
SORE LOSER
Yeah.

Later.
There goes the last of them.

"The Specter Collectors Society."
THAT'S IT!
Gurgazon isn't just going to *escape*. Oh *no*.
GURGAZON IS BRINGING THIS PLACE *DOWN*.
I M WITH YOU
BRINGING *ALL* OF THEM DOWN.
ONE WAY OR ANOTHER!
SMASH
TIME FOR TEA!

Book Two

Author Bio

Ray Fawkes is a critically acclaimed writer and artist based in Toronto, Canada. His work has appeared online and in print around the world, and he is a two-time nominee for a Shuster award as "Outstanding Canadian Comic Book Writer." He ranges in style from dark, visceral horror (*Mnemovore*, *Black Strings*) to slapstick and black humor (*The Apocalipstix*), and has been published by DC/Vertigo, Oni Press, Tor.com, Top Shelf 2.0, White Wolf Publishing, and more.

www.rayfawkes.com

OTHER BOOKS FROM ONI PRESS

APOCALIPSTIX
VOLUME 1
BY RAY FAWKES & CAMERON STEWART
144 PAGES • DIGEST
BLACK AND WHITE
$11.95 US
ISBN 978-1-932664-45-4

COURTNEY CRUMRIN
VOLUME 1: THE NIGHT THINGS
BY TED NAIFEH
128 PAGES • DIGEST
BLACK AND WHITE
$11.95 US
ISBN 978-1-929998-60-9

LOLA
BY J. TORRES AND ELBERT OR
112 PAGES • HARDCOVER
BLACK AND WHITE
$14.95 US
ISBN 978-1-934964-33-0

POLLY AND THE PIRATES, VOLUME 1
BY TED NAIFEH
176 PAGES • DIGEST
BLACK AND WHITE
$11.95 US
ISBN 978-1-932664-46-1

SALT WATER TAFFY, VOLUME 1 -
THE LEGEND OF OLD SALTY
BY MATTHEW LOUX
96 PAGES • DIGEST
BLACK AND WHITE
$5.95 US
ISBN 978-1-932664-94-2

POSSESSIONS
VOLUME 3
THE BETTER HOUSE-TRAP
BY RAY FAWKES

SPRING 2012!

YO GABBA GABBA:
GOOD NIGHT, GABBALAND
BY J. TORRES & MATTHEW LOUX
16 PAGES • BOARD COMIC
FULL COLOR
$7.99 US
ISBN 978-1-934964-56-9

For more information on these and other fine Oni Press comic books and graphic novels, visit www.onipress.com. To find a comic specialty store in your area, call 1-888-COMICBOOK or visit www.comicshops.us.

www.onipress.com